Hanging Baskets

RAY WAITE

Cassell

The Royal Horticultural Society

THE ROYAL HORTICULTURAL SOCIETY

Cassell Educational Limited
Villiers House, 41/47 Strand
London WC2N 5JE
for the Royal Horticultural Society

First published 1995

British Library Cataloguing in Publication Data
A catalogue record of this book is available from the
British Library

ISBN 0–304–32063–3

Photographs by Andrew Lawson, pp. 20, 26, 34, 40,
57; Photos Horticultural, pp. 4, 6, 8, 10, 11, 29,
30(left), 31(left), 33(below), 36, 37, 43, 49, 50, 52, 55,
56, 58, 60, 62; Harry Smith Collection pp. 12, 14, 17,
23, 27, 30(right), 31(right), 33(above), 39, 44, 48, 63

Phototypesetting by RGM Typesetting, Southport

Printed in Hong Kong by Wing King Tong Co. Ltd

Cover: A generously planted hanging basket
includes lobelia, alyssum, *Begonia semperflorens*,
violas, fuchsias and pelargoniums
Back cover: Vibrant colours for a sunny situation:
mixed pelargoniums, nasturtiums and that stalwart
of hanging baskets, trailing lobelia
  Photographs by Eric Crichton
p.1: Lobelias in mixed colours are among the most
reliable plants for hanging baskets (see p.38)
  Photograph by Photos Horticultural

Contents

Introduction   5

Choosing a Hanging Basket   7
  The choice   7
  Suspension   9

Assembling the Basket   13
  Lining the basket   13
  Composts   14
  A globe of flowers   16
  Protection   17
  Planting schemes   18

General Maintenance   19
  Watering   19
  Feeding   21
  Maintaining the display   21
  Pests and diseases   21

Raising Plants   22
  Growing from seed   22
  Growing from cuttings   23

How to Avoid Trouble   25
  Watering   25
  Position   25
  Compost   25
  Hygiene   26
  Winter hanging baskets   26

Plants for Outdoor Hanging Baskets   27

Plants for the Greenhouse and Conservatory   47

Index   64

Introduction

Hanging baskets are one of the most effective and popular forms of decorative gardening today. And with good reason. Those with little or no gardening experience can easily and quickly create a colourful, long-lasting display, and the satisfaction and visual rewards carry on throughout a season.

So often the plants cooperate fully by intertwining artistically and flowing over the edges of the basket with charming and luxuriant abandon. For the strategic positioning of even a single basket, well furnished with plants, can brighten the most unpromising aspect.

The more experienced gardener can experiment, try more unusual plants or emulate old-time cottage gardens which often combined the decorative and the edible. You can even plant hanging baskets as living flower arrangements – striving for drama, for contrast or for a homely effect.

We are all accustomed to the sight of welcoming hanging baskets in the spring and of the traditional explosion of vibrant colour in the summer. More subdued, with all the beauty inherent in that, are hanging baskets for autumn and winter. They are perhaps even more welcome because they are so unexpected in the quiet months.

The greenhouse, the conservatory and the home all provide a variety of situations for hanging baskets, which was appreciated by the Victorians. Small wall pots, a modification of the hanging basket, are also very effective. This kind of small-scale gardening enjoyed by the Victorians has experienced a very strong revival in recent years. As a result, plants, containers, liners and composts are readily to hand in garden centres, although some gardeners enjoy propagating their own plants, and seeking out unusual containers or making their own.

Choose your season, the position, the container, then the plants for that position and the compost for those plants. The plants themselves offer a range of colour, height, texture, perfume, while the foliage contributes shape and texture as well as the necessary foil for the flowers. Over the years, those plants recommended on pages 27 to 63 have proved reliable and have given me consistently good results. However, never be afraid to try out different plants

Many orchids grow well in baskets, in particular *Coelogyne cristata* (see p. 53)

A mass display of variegated nasturtium 'Alaska' (see p. 45)

and new cultivars that take your fancy.

Hanging baskets bring life and colour to every situation. In return they demand very regular watering and feeding. The need for careful and consistent watering cannot be over-emphasized. Even if it has rained, the foliage may have thrown off the water, so vigilence is required. But this is a small price to pay for the sight of a miniature garden, thriving in mid-air, to cheer all who pass by.

—— Choosing a Hanging Basket ——

Hanging baskets give excellent value and are the easiest way of livening up most situations provided it is understood that they demand very regular watering and feeding. This is especially true of the more traditional type constructed of wire. Even though the solid plastic bowl types, complete with reservoir, are less likely to dry out so rapidly, attention to adequate irrigation is still the main factor required to bring success. Nothing looks worse than a poorly furnished basket or one that contains drought-ridden plants struggling to keep alive; indeed, it is better to have no container at all.

THE CHOICE

Before choosing a hanging basket first consider whether it is for outdoors, greenhouse or home and what plants are to be grown. There is a very wide choice.

The traditional basket is made from galvanized wire with the strands either running spirally or so arranged as to form small diamond or square holes. The latter is usually best for planting into the sides. It is common for wire to be plastic coated to extend the useful life of the basket.

The newer types of baskets are more often than not made with square holes and flat bottoms which make planting easier as the basket is held much steadier; this is also convenient when it can be stood straight on to a greenhouse bench to encourage the intitial establishment of the plants. Sizes range from 15 cm (6 in.) up to 45 cm (18 in.) in diameter or even larger.

Plastic hanging baskets with an open mesh similar to those contstructed from wire are also available.

Solid plastic types are best described as hanging pots. They come in various sizes, with the largest being about 30 cm (12 in.) in diameter, and are available in different colours, white, green and terracotta being the most usual. Some solid hanging baskets are ornamental and may appeal to those wishing to have an indoor display. However, it is more than likely that one fitted with a reservoir at the base will be desirable, as this not only helps to irrigate the plants but saves excess water from dripping on to the floor. Reservoirs are held either internally or attached beneath the base. A further modification is where the solid plastic basket has

The plume-like sprays of *Asparagus densiflorus* 'Sprengeri' (see p. 51)

planting pockets in the sides so that it can be more readily furnished with plants.

Solid terracotta pots are particularly useful in the home especially when they are suspended with macramé or a single strong chain; even then it may be necessary to place a drip tray on the floor when watering. Because there are no drainage holes, watering must be done with care to ensure the compost does not become waterlogged. Alternatively use these to hide a plainer pot with drainage holes.

Compressed fibre bowls held in a wire cradle are a simple type of hanging basket suitable only for out of doors or the greenhouse.

Slatted wooden baskets can look attractive in their own right as they are made from natural material. They are particularly suitable for orchids and bromeliads which do not need much moisture in the potting compost. They are also suitable for growing ferns. Some can be bought in a kit form and are simple to assemble, others purchased ready-made from specialist suppliers. They are relatively expensive.

SUSPENSION

Whatever method is selected to suspend the basket it is necessary to ensure that it is strong enough, especially if the container is large as, inevitably, it will become increasingly heavy after watering and as the plants grow larger. A novel method of displaying hanging baskets is to suspend one basket below another. This can look particularly effective if the uppermost basket is slightly smaller. It is wise to inspect the fixing points on the baskets to make sure they are adequate. (The size of the bracket should be commensurate with the size of the basket.)

Chains have been used for many years but must be strongly made: those with closed links are the most satisfactory.

Galvanized wire is also used but is aesthetically not as pleasing, although this is less of a consideration when plants are likely to mask the chain.

Solid plastic chains are found on most of the plastic types of basket. These chains either clip on to a specially formed groove or slot into holes in the rim. However, plastic 'chains' on cheap pots are likely to break.

Create a more abundant display by suspending one basket below another, but take care that the supporting structure and attachment are strong enough to bear the weight

Macramé, already mentioned, is for the home or conservatory. It is decorative but somewhat heavy in form, therefore any plant in a macramé hanger must be a bold subject so that it is in balance with this means of suspension.

Wall hangers, a modification of hanging basket, are made from plastic-covered wire or solid plastic. They are fixed on a wall with screws, and are especially useful in a narrow space. Wall hangers grouped with hanging baskets can create a very striking display.

Brackets

A hanging basket needs a strong bracket. Suitable brackets are usually metal and often painted black. They are available in packs with screws and proprietary plugs. It will be necessary to re-paint brackets regularly to keep them in good condition, as they can soon go rusty and will not look pleasing. The weight of the basket filled with moist compost and plants is considerable, so it is essential that the bracket be securely screwed to the wall. Holes should be drilled and plugged into the brickwork to receive an adequate length screw, at least 6 cm (2½ in.) long. For heavy or large baskets longer screws will be necessary. A novel way of suspending hanging baskets is to screw several brackets into a strong wooden upright so that an all-round display is provided. It is possible to achieve a similar effect using small wall hangers or hanging pots. Where hooks are to be used, say, on a wooden pergola or archway they must also be strong and securely fixed.

Wall hangers with *Pelargonium* Balcon Selection in combination with white campanulas

Grouped wall baskets with verbena, chlorophytum and silvery lotus

Spring-loaded suspension systems

To make watering and general maintenance easy it is possible to obtain special spring-loaded suspension systems so that the hanging basket can be lowered to a convenient height and then automatically returned to its display position. Remember, these systems are only capable of supporting a limited weight which must be calculated by weighing the planted basket after watering. Remember too that a hanging basket completely saturated with water may exceed the recommended load which is indicated on the suspension mechanism. In an exposed position the suspension cord may tangle in the wind.

A strong bracket supports a basket filled with mixed nasturtiums

Assembling the Basket

Setting up a hanging basket is a satisfying task but to achieve this the necessary plants and materials need to be assembled together before the work commences. Firstly decide on the best sized container for the job. A round-based basket can be held upright by placing it in an empty flower pot or bucket, which will in any case facilitate planting in the sides. Flat-bottomed baskets sit quite steadily on the working surface but they are easier to plant if raised on an inverted flower pot.

LINING THE BASKET

Open-mesh baskets require some sort of lining to retain the potting compost.

Moss has been used traditionally, and can still be purchased specially selected and graded. For appearance and ease of planting through the sides there is nothing quite comparable. It gives a very nice finish, although when the plants are well grown they will completely cover the basket anyhow. The conservation issue has made many people turn to alternative lining materials.

Solid liners made from compressed recycled paper or fibre are perfectly adequate and if holes are bored in the sides (an old potato peeler is an ideal tool) the plant roots can be pushed through.

Foam plastic liners are slightly easier to use. These are cut out in such a way that they readily take up the configuration of the basket. As they are made with slits it is possible to squeeze roots through carefully.

Impregnated cardboard liners, some of which have a disc of fibrous material that is claimed to act as a water reservoir, are of a similar design to those made of foam plastic and can also be slit to accommodate plants.

Coconut fibre interwoven with a loose plastic mesh is yet another type of liner. Coconut fibre seems to be extremely durable.

Proprietary woven plastic shading material makes a very simple-to-use lining for a basket. It can be bought in variouis mesh sizes. This material is easily moulded to the shape of the basket and, as holes are simple to make, planting in the sides is no problem.

Plastic sheeting can be used but choose black in preference to green, and certainly not white. The latter can be extremely obtrusive unless well-enveloped with plant growth. Plastic sheeting is also good as an inner liner when using moss and will help to retain moisture.

COMPOSTS

Proprietary peat and coconut-fibre potting composts are ideal for hanging baskets but remember that both, particularly the former, can dry out quite rapidly and are often difficult to completely saturate again. The light weight compared to that of loam-based composts, such as John Innes, is obviously important as any reduction in load must be an advantage. Proprietary hanging-basket composts are available, but these are peat-based and will need regular watering.

Planting a hanging basket should be done in stages, usually working from the bottom up. If moss is being used as a liner for a wire basket, place enough moss to line the bottom third. The 'basin' of moss is filled with moist potting compost which is then firmed. The sides of the basket can be planted either by inserting the root-balls of selected plants through the wire mesh at the side from the outside, or the top growth is brought together in a paper sleeve and pushed through from the inside. The type and quantity of growth will dictate the method to be chosen. Then prepare a further

Regular feeding is important to ensure good crops of parsley and tomatoes

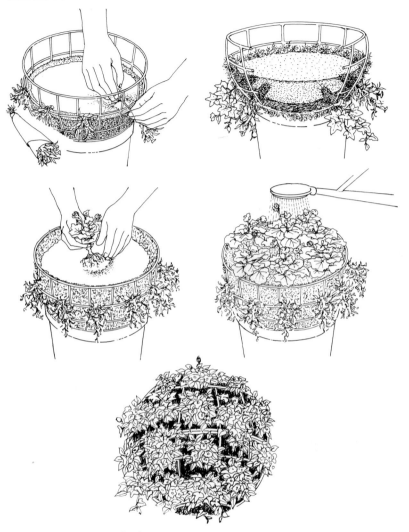

Planting up a hanging basket

1 Steady the basket on a flowerpot or bucket while planting up. Partially line and fill with compost. Insert plants through the sides. This task is made easier if the young plants are first wrapped in a sleeve of paper
2 Add more lining material and compost as you plant the layers
3 Before planting the top of the basket, ensure there is a good rim of lining material
4 Plant the top of the basket generously, water and keep the basket out of direct sunlight until the plants have established themselves
5 A globe of blossom can be achieved by inverting one basket onto another and wiring them together securely. The plants will soon cover the frames

section of the basket by mossing to two-thirds its depth and continue planting as above. Finally, moss the whole basket making sure that there is a good rim of moss standing above the top edge to retain water. More compost is consolidated lightly below rim level to allow for sufficient water to be applied. Complete planting at the top, then water thoroughly.

A good maxim when planting up a basket – indeed any container – is to plant generously. Obviously there will be some limit to the quantity of the plants used, but nothing is worse than a sparsely furnished planting leaving the basket itself dominant. If some subjects ultimately become inundated there is no need to worry, for, in practice, plants tend to struggle for their own space and any intermingling gives a pleasing massed effect. Selection of plants and colour combinations is a personal choice but some ideas for a large basket in summer and winter/spring are given on page 18.

It is especially important to plant winter and autumn baskets generously, as the plants will not grow so much and spill over the sides as they do in spring and summer.

Planting a basket lined with a preformed liner is slightly more straightforward than using moss. Place the liner in position and, if necessary, cut slits to allow planting through the sides. Plant with care so as not to damage leaves or roots. It is advisable to wrap the plants in a sleeve of paper before pushing them through the slit. Once the plant is in position, remove the paper and continue as described for a mossed basket, above.

Plastic sheeting or woven plastic is laid in the basket and cut with a generous margin of overlap at the top. Holes for side-planting are simple to cut. Once the basket is fully planted, the edges of the lining material can be trimmed or tucked in to make a neat edge (soon covered by the planting).

A GLOBE OF FLOWERS

A variation is to invert one basket on top of another to form a sphere. First, the lower basket is filled and the bottom and sides planted as described above, before a second basket is fastened securely on top with wires. The upper basket is then planted by pushing first compost, then moss through the mesh, planting the sides as you go until it is full. The top does not need to be planted as the plants will grow up naturally to complete the globe. This is rather fiddley but the result can be stunning when a single species or cultivar is used, such as *Begonia sempervirens*, busy lizzies (*Impatiens walleriana*), or *Viola × wittrockiana*.

Left: A globe of violas. Right: Mixed herbs for a foliage display

PROTECTION

Hanging baskets planted for winter and spring display need the protection of a cold greenhouse or sheltered porch during very hard weather. Those destined for outdoor summer display benefit greatly from an early start under glass. This means that plants will have to be produced well beforehand so that they are sufficiently established ready for planting in April in a warm greenhouse. If they can be gradually hardened off so much the better, for if growth becomes too soft weather damage can easily result once placed in their flowering situation. In any case care must be taken to guard against late frosts and if these are a threat it will be wise to bring the baskets under cover or drape them with newspaper or a specially manufactured 'horticultural fleece' at night.

PLANTING SCHEMES

Planting schemes and colour combinations are very much a personal choice, but some summer and winter/spring suggestions for large baskets are given below as a guide.

Suggestions for winter/spring baskets

12△ Polyanthus
  4○ *Euonymus fortunei* 'Emerald Gaiety'
  5✳ *Ajuga reptans* 'Burgundy Glow'

  5△ *Myosotis* 'Blue Basket'
  3○ *Hedera helix* 'Buttercup'
12✳ *Narcissus* 'Hawera'

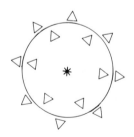

14△ Viola (pansies) also two rows planted in the sides
  1✳ *Aucuba japonica*

Suggestions for summer baskets

3○ *Pelargonium* 'Plantinum'
3✳ *Helichrysum petiolare* 'Sulphurea'
6△ *Lobelia* 'Light Blue Basket'
    alternating in two rows with
6 + pink petunias

4○ *Begonia semperflorens* 'Frilly Red'
5✳ *Nemesia fruticans*
5△ *Calceolaria rugosa* 'Sunshine'
    alternating in two rows with
5 + *Lotus bertholetii*

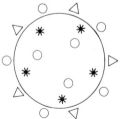

5✳ *Scaevola aemula*
8○ Ivy-leaved *Pelargonium* 'Pink Mini Cascade'
5△ *Felicia amelloides* 'Variegata'
    alternating in two rows with
    Pelargonium 'Pink Mini Cascade'

18

To keep hanging baskets looking good for as long as possible give them regular, often daily, attention. Watering and feeding are of paramount importance. Removing spent flowers and any dead leaves keeps the display well groomed. Some judicious pruning of over-vigorous occupants will prevent them overwhelming neighbours of more modest growth.

WATERING

Watering is the key factor in maintaining good hanging baskets. It is not uncommon in the height of the growing season, in hot dry and especially windy weather, for them to dry out to such an extent that they need to be watered more than once a day. Because of the exposed position of hanging containers, they are bound to be vulnerable to excessive desiccation. It follows, then, that a larger container is slightly less prone to this particular problem, but the increased number of plants will also make their demand on moisture constant.

Place hanging baskets to make irrigation as easy as possible. Ensure that, once watered, any excess that drips through does not become a nuisance.

It may be possible to use a watering-can, especially if the basket is suspended on an adjustable system (see p. 11). A long-spouted can sometimes can be used if it is held above head height with one hand grasping the actual spout. Where hanging baskets are fairly low a garden hose will suffice. Make the end rigid by tying it to a stout bamboo cane, so a greater height can be reached. Alternatively, a length of metal pipe bent over at the top and attached to the end of a hose is very useful.

A hand-held device that delivers water using a pumping action is on the market and is suitable if you have a small number of baskets. However where there are a large number of baskets, it is possible to set up some sort of drip system. A length of main tubing can be so situated that strategically placed nozzles or secondary tubing is positioned over or near a basket. A more sophisticated version could include a timing device so that water is switched on and off automatically, but for most people the operation of a tap turned on and off by hand will be satisfactory.

Plants in hanging baskets need regular feeding and deadheading

In recent years the inclusion of a special water-retaining polymer in the potting compost has been advocated. These polymers are incorporated as granules and are capable of absorbing a large quantity of water. Results are variable as, to be effective, it seems the roots of the plants need to penetrate the polymer, but many gardeners consider them of value.

Do not forget that hanging baskets need to be watered in autumn and winter. Test the compost regularly to check on the level of moisture.

FEEDING

Very much linked to watering is the supplementary feeding of plants in hanging baskets in summer. The fertilizer incorporated in potting composts is **not** sufficient to carry plants through the growing season, as much will have been leached away by the many waterings and this must be replaced. Liquid feeding is the easiest form of fertilizer to apply as it is possible to give a very dilute concentration at every watering. Where a number of containers are to be maintained a dilutor fixed to a hose is useful as the concentrated feed is picked up by the displacement at pre-set rates and delivered through a hoze nozzle in the normal way.

A balanced feed is recommended but some manufacturers make specially formulated fertilizers. Feeds with a higher potash element, such as tomato fertilisers, will obviate very lush growth and tend to give more and better flower colour, but those with an emphasis on nitrogen will give more growth and prolong flowering. At least one supplier makes sachets of slow-release fertilizer, which are placed at the bottom of the hanging basket at planting time. Tablets of slow-release fertilizer can also be used, pushed into the surface of the compost. But on balance it is likely that the regular liquid feeds give better results.

Outdoor displays of plants for autumn and winter, in general, do not need feeding. Basket displays hanging indoors, or in a well-heated conservatory or greenhouse benefit from an occasional feed during autumn and winter months.

MAINTAINING THE DISPLAY

Regular watering and feeding are essential to keep a display going and to keep it healthy. In order to extend the flowering life of many plants it pays to remove spent flower heads and this also cleans up and improves the appearance of the display. Decaying foliage should also be removed at the same time. If it is possible, turn the display at regular intervals so that plants can grow evenly.

PESTS AND DISEASES

Generally speaking, there is little problem from pests and disease. However, greenfly (aphids) and mildew can be a nuisance at times. They are easily controlled by applying an appropriate proprietary pesticide, or in the latter case a fungicide, used according to the manufacturers' instructions.

Raising Plants

It is possible to buy a wide range of suitable plants from a nursery or garden centre but many people enjoy propagating their own plants from seed or cuttings. Most plants can be raised in a warm greenhouse where it is possible to maintain a night temperature of about 10°C (50°F). This is ideal especially if the greenhouse is equipped with a heated propagating case, but it is surprising how many plants can be raised utilizing the airing cupboard and/or window sills.

GROWING FROM SEED

The easiest and cheapest way of raising plants in large numbers is from seed. Use a proprietary seed compost to fill suitably sized containers/pots, seed trays or. moulded plastic or polystyrene cellular trays. Lightly consolidate, level the surface and water thoroughly. Allow the compost to drain before sowing seed. It is wasteful of valuable propagating space and compost to use too large a container for a small amount of seed; conversely, seeds should be given adequate space to prevent possible damping-off and the seedlings becoming weak and spindly.

After sowing the seed must be covered with a light dressing of compost which should also be gently firmed and given a level surface. It is true that some plants germinate much more readily and evenly if the seed is left uncovered, petunias and begonias for example. But as a rule of thumb cover to a depth equal approximately to four times the diameter of the seed. After sowing the compost must be kept moist at all times and as a precaution against any damping-off disease an initial soaking with a solution of Cheshunt Compound is wise. Cover the sown container(s) with either black polythene, brown paper, or several thicknesses of newspaper except, of course, those subjects where light is stipulated on the packet, and, if possible, set in a heated propagating case at the temperature recommended on the seed packet until germination takes place.

As soon as the seed has germinated remove the plastic or paper covering to allow the seedlings to develop. Once large enough to handle, ideally at seed-leaf stage and certainly before developing too many leaves, prick them out into plant trays, modular inserts or small pots to be grown on ready for planting up.

Three wall pots, arranged in tiers, planted with petunias and lobelias

GROWING FROM CUTTINGS

Most perennial plants can be readily propagated from stem cuttings of fairly soft or semi-ripe material. A heated propagating unit is invaluable but many plants can be rooted in a pot placed in a polythene bag. Keep the polythene from touching the cuttings by means of three or four sticks pushed into the compost. Stand the pot of cuttings on a suitable window sill. The practise of rooting cuttings in water is not recommended as considerbale difficulty can be experienced when attempting to establish them in a potting compost.

Cutting material need not be too long. For example, pelargonium cuttings should be 7.5–10 cm (3–4 in.); scaevola about 5 cm (2 in.); and *Helichrysum petiolare* about 7.5 cm (3 in.). Some of the lower leaves should be removed cleanly using a razor blade or sharp knife. Then the stem is cut across just below a node (a leaf

23

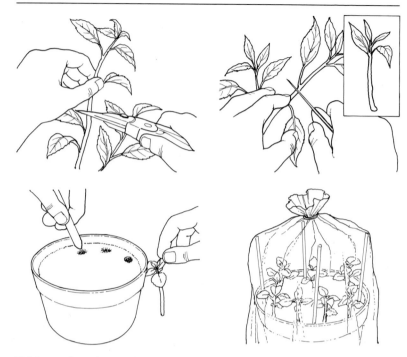

Taking and rooting cuttings
1 Take a cutting from a non-flowering shoot
2 Trim just below a leaf joint and remove the lower leaves
3 Insert cuttings round the edge of a pot and water in
4 Put the pot of cuttings in a polythene bag to maintain a moist atmosphere until rooting has taken place

junction). An open gritty compost consisting of equal parts of sharp sand and coco-fibre or peat gives the best results and it is unlikely that rooting hormone will be required. Choose a suitably sized container for the number of cuttings required. For instance, a 9 cm (3½ in.) pot will take about four cuttings of an ivy-leaved pelargonium or six cuttings of *Lobelia richardii*, while a 13 cm (5 in.) pot will take six or seven ivy-leaved pelargoniums, but ten or twelve cuttings of the lobelia. Insert the cuttings round the edge of the pot and water thoroughly. Lightly shade the cuttings with newspaper or netting to obviate flagging; once the cuttings have rooted sufficiently and show signs of new growth, this shading should be removed. Once growth is underway the young plants can be potted on into a small pot, seed tray or cellular tray filled with potting compost and grown on until it is time to plant up the hanging basket.

How to Avoid Trouble

WATERING

Regular watering is essential, therefore plan how you intend to water when you choose the position. Hanging baskets should be:
- Easy to reach
- Checked regularly for drying out
- Watered several times a day in a very sunny position. Try not to water in the sun, for the leaves may scorch. Morning and evening are the best times.
- Watered in out-of-reach positions by attaching a bamboo pole to the end of the hose to make it rigid to give you greater height. Or arrange a pulley system for the basket, or a pump for regular watering.
- Watered by a reliable neighbour at holiday-time, or
  - Stand baskets in a shady and sheltered position
  - Water thoroughly before leaving
  - Rig up drip feed system with a water reservoir nearby
  - Try adding moisture-retaining granules to the compost

POSITION

Hanging baskets are, by their very nature, exposed to drying and buffeting by the wind, damaging to both plants and container
- Avoid very exposed positions, such as a 'wind-tunnel' drive
- Remember that the higher the basket, the more exposed it is
- Choose mainly low and compact plants, such as short-growing daffodils, pansies
- Also, place baskets where they won't be bumped by people or doors.

Hanging baskets are usually close to buildings where there are often extremes of light and shade during the day.
- If too shady, paint walls white or a pale colour or position mirrors to reflect more light
- If too sunny, for instance in a conservatory, deflect some of the sun with blinds, netting or matting.

COMPOST

- Use the right compost for the plants, eg, lime-free or ericaceous soil for acid-loving plants such as heathers

White walls are a good foil for containers of mixed plants and colours

- The compost should be sterile, a free-draining mixture, but reasonably water-retentive, and lightweight.

HYGIENE

- Choose healthy plants
- Use clean and sterilised pots and soil
- Water and feed as required to maintain optimum health
- Dispose of diseased parts or plants
- Hand pick and dispose of larger pests

WINTER HANGING BASKETS

- Containers should be frost-proof
- Plants should be hardy
- Pinch off dead leaves and foliage
- Leave snow on basket, as it gives protection
- Check to see if soil has dried out; water during warm periods.

Plants for Outdoor Hanging Baskets

In some of the major flower shows special competitions for hanging baskets are included giving rise to many novel but sometimes not always very practical ideas. However all are interesting, with plantings ranging from succulents to vegetables and even fruit. Several are worthy a try if something a little out of the ordinary is desired. For example, tomato 'Tumbler' makes an ideal subject as the red fruits are not only decorative but palatable. Cucumbers 'Bush Champion' and 'Patio Pik' with their small fruits and short trailing stems are another choice.

Several herbs can also be used as once again they are both attractive and utilitarian. Various thymes, marjoram, balm and parsley are recommended. Even the strong-growing mints and sages can also be considered, but it must be appreciated that they cannot reach their full potential growing in a basket.

The obvious choice of fruit is the strawberry, especially when

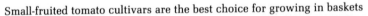

Small-fruited tomato cultivars are the best choice for growing in baskets

protection is available so that an early crop can be harvested. 'Sweetheart' is a cultivar that can, in fact, be raised from seed sown in early spring in a heated propagating case.

When selecting plants always bear in mind the position (sun/shade, sheltered/exposed) and the visual effect you require. The plants listed below are main-stay subjects for hanging baskets. They are all readily available from retail sources, either as seed or as established plants. The usual method of propagation is indicated in each entry, as is their habit of growth – upright or trailing – their main use and most appropriate growing situation. Filler plants are those that intermingle well, their slender stems pushing between the growth of other plants to give a well-furnished appearance to any container.

Ageratum houstonianum Although this popular annual bedding plant is generally too compact to be successful in a hanging basket, the tall growing cultivar 'Tall Blue' can be considered for inclusion in a large planting. The fluffy blue flower heads intermingle with other subjects and, although by no means trailing, when planted in the centre or sides a bold effect is achieved without being over-powering. Seed should be sown February in gentle heat. Sun; upright; side or top.

Argyranthemum frutescens (formerly *Chrysanthemum frutescens*) Commonly called the marguerite or Paris daisy, this is another plant best suited to a large hanging basket. It has a profusion of white daisy-like flowers, but some cultivars, such as 'Mary Wootton', have pink cushion-like centres. Two yellow-flowered agyranthemums are available: A. leucanthemum has deeper coloured flowers compared to A. 'Jamaica Primrose'. Propagation is by cuttings in autumn or early spring. Sun; upright; top.

Aucuba japonica This hardy evergreen shrub seems at first sight to be a most unlikely subject to be included in a basket, but very young plants particularly the variegated A. japonica 'Variegata' and A. japonica 'Crotonifolia' make good central plants in a winter display. Sun or shade; upright; top or central position.

Begonia There are a number of begonias suitable for hanging baskets. Among them *Begonia pendula* is an excellent choice, with flowers of pink, red or orange held on pendulous stems. Dormant tubers can be bought and started into growth in warmth in spring. Seed needs to be sown in winter and requires a temperature of around 23°C (75°F) to germinate. The tiny seedlings must be handled with great care and grown on in warmth early in the year.

Argyranthemum 'Jamaica Primrose'

Semi-shade; trailing; side or top.

Begonia semperflorens is probably the most popular of the fibrous-rooted begonias. There are many cultivars available with masses of small flowers produced over a very long period; 'Frilly Pink', 'Frilly Red' and 'Pink Avalanche' are particularly recommended. Seed should be sown in January and germinated at 23°C (75°F). Sun or shade; upright; top.

Begonia sutherlandii has small orange flowers and seems to be equally at home out of doors as well as under glass. In winter the stems die back to the tuber which should be stored dry and in a frost-free place. Small bulbils form in the leaf axils and these can also be stored and used to propagate more plants in the spring. Shade; semi-trailing; side or top (see p. 50).

Bidens ferulifolia Numerous golden yellow flowers are formed on trailing slender stems making an ideal 'filler' plant. Flowering is continuous over a long period in sun or light shade. Stem cuttings should be taken in the autumn. Sun; semi-trailing; side, top or filler.

Brachycome iberidifolia The Swan River daisy has deep blue or white flowers and is in bloom continuously throughout the summer. Sow seed in warmth in early spring. Sun; semi-trailing; side, top or filler.

Calceolaria rugosa The yellow flowers, shaped like small pouches, are held on fairly slender stems. Happy in sun or light shade and flowers continuously throughout the summer. This plant intermingles well with other plants and never becomes too dominant. Seed should be sown in February in gentle heat, but if larger plants are required a sowing can be made in August for planting the following year. Shade; trailing; side or top.

Campanula Some of the newer introductions of hardy perennial *Campanula carpatica*, such as 'Bellissimo', make fine subjects with their large blue or white bell-shaped flowers. Seed needs to be sown in early spring in warmth so that plants will flower by late May.

Campanula isophylla, the trailing bellflower, has blue or white flowers and is ideal for smaller baskets. It is easily grown and has a long flowering period in either sun or partial shade. 'Stella Blue' and 'Stella White' can be raised from seed sown in the previous summer before planting but cuttings can be rooted in autumn or spring. Shade; trailing; side or top.

Left: *Calceolaria rugosa*. Right: *Campanula isophylla*

Chlorophytum comosum 'Variegatum' Commonly called the spider plant, this robust subject is suitable for outdoor baskets in the summer. It looks best grown in a large hanging basket display where its bold variegated foliage and flower spikes with tufts of plantlets at their extremities can set off other plants. The spider plant is probably at its best when grown alone in a conservatory or home. Propagation is by division or stem plantlets. Sun or shade; semi-trailing; side or top (see p. 37).

Convolvulus The beautiful perennial *Convolvulus sabatius* is a trailing plant that never becomes overpowering with other plants but is equally an excellent single subject for a small or medium-sized hanging basket. The plant generally grown has mid-blue flowers but pink forms are known; however *C. althaeoides* is a good pink-flowered species and although not making quite such a bold plant as *C. sabatius*, is excellent. Neither are reliably hardy and should be propagated from cuttings in the autumn. Sun; trailer; side or top.

Left: *Convolvulus sabatius*. Right: *Dorotheanthus bellidiformis*, often sold as mesembryanthemum (see p. 32)

Dorotheanthus bellidiformis This is usually listed in seed catalogues as *Mesembryanthemum criniflorum*. The daisy-like flowers come in a wide range of colours. It is a useful addition in smaller baskets, but is less successful in a larger mixed planting. A position in full sun will ensure that the flowers stay open. The cultivars 'Magic Carpet' and 'Sparkles' are recommended. Seed should be sown in heat in early spring and the seedlings pricked off into small pots to minimise root disturbance when planting up. Sun; semi-trailing; side or top.

Erica carnea (Winter heath) This makes an excellent subject for the increasing popularity of winter-interest hanging baskets. 'Springwood Pink' and 'Springwood White' are particularly suitable as they are less compact than other cultivars and tend to flop down over the basket sides. Cuttings can be inserted in summer but some time will elapse before they become usable plants. Increasing by layering will hasten production, but in practice it is easier to buy established plants. Sun; upright; side or top.

Erigeron karwinskianus This hardy plant can be easily flowered in a few months from seed sown in heat in spring. The cultivar 'Profusion' is now becoming popular; its daisy-like flowers tinged with pink literally smother the plant. As a 'filler', it is ideal. Sun; trailing; side, top or filler.

Euonymus fortunei A hardy, evergreen shrub which in due course spreads and trails. However it is usually planted as a fairly young plant for winter display. 'Emerald 'n' Gold' and 'Emerald Gaiety' are, respectively, gold and silver variegated cultivars. Cuttings will root readily at almost any time of the year. Sun or shade; upright; side or top.

Felicia amelloides Cascading, bright blue daisy-like flowers throughout the summer. *F. amelloides* 'Variegata' makes an interesting addition in any planting. Best in full sunshine. Propagate by cuttings in autumn or early spring. Sun; trailer; side or top.

Fuchsia These well-known plants have mostly flowers that hang down making them ideal basket plants. However the trailing cultivars are even better, as their slender stems cascade and intermingle with other plants. As a single subject they are perfect and although performing well out-of-doors they grow to perfection under glass, especially the double-flowered cultivars. Cuttings should be rooted in the autumn or early spring and then potted off into small pots so that the root-ball is not too large but remains a

Above: *Felicia amelloides* 'Variegate'. Below: *Fuchsia* 'Auntie Jinks' (see p. 34)

manageable size for planting up. There are many cultivars available but the following have performed particularly well when on trial at Wisley. Semi-shade or shade; upright or trailing; central, top or side position.

'Auntie Jinks' although fairly compact trails nicely; the cream and pink tubes and sepals set off the purplish corolla.

'Autumnale' is another excellent foliage cultivar, a very old introduction but still holding its own having golden foliage with orange and red variegation. It does, however, pay to keep the growing tips pinched back regularly in order to retain the intense variegation.

'La Campanella' is a delightful semi-double with small flowers. The tube and sepals are deep red, the corolla deep purple.

'Cascade', introduced in 1937 is excellent producing a mass of basically red flowers.

'Golden Marinka' has bright red flowers shading to deep pink which contrasts very well with the golden foliage. 'Marinka' itself, with all-green foliage, is also worth growing.

'Pink Marshmallow' is as attractive as its name, the large double flowers of soft pink making a spectacular basket.

'Red Spider' is mainly red and makes a fine specimen.

'Swingtime' has large fully double flowers giving an overall

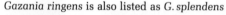

Gazania ringens is also listed as *G. splendens*

effect of deep pink.

'**Tom West**' is well worth growing for its striking variegated foliage alone; its small red flowers are an added attraction.

'**Troika**' has very much smaller blossoms and is similar in colour to 'La Campanella'.

Gazania ringens A sun-loving plant best suited to smaller hanging baskets. Large daisy-like flowers come in shades of cream, yellow, orange, carmine, pink and bronze. Some of the best recent introductions are 'Sundance', 'Chansonette and 'Harlequin Hybrid' with a full range of colours which can be raised from seed, whereas double-flowered 'Yellow Buttons', the variegated leaved kinds 'Vimmers Variegated' and 'Variegata', and 'Silver Beauty' must be propagated from cuttings in the autumn. Sun; upright; side or top.

Glechoma hederacea '**Variegata**' The variegated ground ivy has white-blotched leaves and long, slender, trailing stems which can sometimes look out of balance on robust plants. However, used with care it can give an excellent effect. Although quite hardy, cuttings are best rooted in the spring in warmth. Sun; top; side.

Hedera helix (Ivy) The many cultivars of the common ivy are superb for winter and spring display. Being, in the main, quite unaffected by hard weather the glossy foliage, often with strong variegation, sets off other plants. Ivies are particularly at home in a shady spot. Cuttings root quite readily at most times of the year. Shade; trailing; side or top.

Hebe × franciscana '**Variegata**' Although not reliably hardy this evergreen shrub makes a pleasing main subject for winter display in a favoured position. The silver variegated foliage mixes well with other plants. It is also useful as part of a summer planting. Propagation is by stem cuttings rooted in spring and summer. Sun; upright; central.

Helichrysum microphyllum (*Plectostachys serpyllifolia*) This is a small-leaved half-hardy perennial. The silver grey foliage is held on fairly short stems and is not too rampant. If planted in the sides of a basket it will trail down approximately 30 cm (12 in.). Sun; trailing; side and top.

Helichrysum petiolare This species and its cultivars 'Sulphurea', with yellow foliage, and 'Variegata' all have woolly leaves and can be quite rampant but are perfect for a bold effect. The growth intertwines with other plants to give a pleasing effect but some judicious

pruning may be necessary to keep the plant within bounds. Propagate by stem cuttings in autumn or spring. Sun; trailing; side or top.

Impatiens walleriana Busy Lizzies have rightly become very popular as they flower continuously in shade or sun. They come into bloom quite early in the year and only finish when frosted in the autumn. Colours range from light purple, red, pink, lilac and white and some such as the 'Zig Zag' series have striped flowers. Seed requires a germination temperature of 21°C (70°F) in light and high humidity in early spring. Semi-shade; upright; side or top.

Ipomoea 'Minibar Rose' Morning glories are much too rampant to make successful basket plants except for this cultivar with its variegated foliage and rose red flowers with a white margin. Although it can be grown outdoors it perhaps performs even better in the greenhouse or conservatory. Sow seed in heat during April. Sun; trailing; side, top or filler.

Opposite: *Lantana montevidensis* (see p. 38)
Above: Mixed impatiens with variegated ivy and chlorophytum

Lamium maculatum A handsomely marked foliage plant with purple, pink or white leaves quite hardy; so a useful 'filler' for a winter/spring display basket. There are silver- and gold-leaved forms which are very attractive. They are easily propagated by stem cuttings rooted in spring or summer. Sun; semi-trailing; side or top.

Lantana camara A fairly tender woody perennial that has white, yellow, orange, red or pink flat flower heads. At one time seed was readily available but it is now easier to obtain plants and rooted cuttings taken from the softer green growth in the autumn. L. montevidensis has lilac flowers and is a less strong grower; the stems are also more slender. Both species intermingle with other plants extremely well and bloom throughout the summer and early autumn. Sun; semi-trailing; side, top or filler.

Lathyrus odoratus Some of the dwarf forms of sweet pea can be included in hanging baskets provided the seed pods are regularly removed so that the flowering period is extended as long as possible. The cultivars 'Knee Hi', 'Jet Set', 'Bijou', 'Snoopea' and 'Supersnoop' are all recommended. Sow seed in February in gentle heat. Sun; semi-trailing; side or top.

Lobelia erinus The trailing forms of this ever-popular plant are invaluable; there is a tendency, however, for flowering to diminish as the season progresses especially in hot weather. 'Light Blue Basket', 'Blue Basket', 'Sapphire' and 'Red Cascade' are all good and can be raised from seed sown in heat in February. Semi-shade; upright or trailing; side, top or filler.

A deep blue cultivar sold as L. richardsonii is becoming more popular but as the flowers are sterile it is necessary to take cuttings in early spring or autumn. Semi-shade; trailing; side, top or filler (see p. 1).

Lotus The silvery fine-leaved Lotus berthelotii has long trailing stems with orange beak-like flowers which can appear during spring and summer but it is for the foliage that it is grown primarily. 'Kew Form' has red flowers. L. × maculatus is less silvery and has red and yellow flowers. Stem cuttings should be rooted in autumn or spring. Sun; trailing; side.

Mimulus (Monkey musk) The musk has been a favourite for many years. New hybrids such as 'Malibu' and 'Calypso' have cream, orange, red and yellow flowers. Mimulus require moist conditions so a sheltered, semi-shaded position is necessary to give satisfactory results. Seed is sown in February in gentle warmth. Semi-shade; upright; side or top.

'Viva', a cultivar of *Mimulus moschatus*

Muscari armeniacum (Grape hyacinth) These are some of the most free flowering of the spring bulbs and when mass planted in a hanging basket give a vivid blue splash of colour during April and early May. Sun; upright; side or top.

Nemesia Colourful hybrids of this delightful South African annual can be used to good effect as the fairly slender stems intermingle well with other plants; this particularly applies to a species whose name is somewhat in doubt but seems to be sold commonly as *N. fruticans* 'Joan Wilder'. Unlike the hybrids which are raised from seed sown in March, the latter is propagated from cuttings rooted in the autumn or spring. Lilac-pink flowers are held on fairly stiff slender stems and are produced over a very long season which can be extended by trimming old flowering growth. The hybrids have cream, yellow, orange and red flowers – 'Carnival', 'Funfair' and 'Tapestry'. 'Blue Gem' is clear blue. Sun; upright; top or filler.

Myosotis sylvatica (Forget-me-not) Although more commonly planted in window boxes and urns forget-me-nots can give a pleasing display in hanging baskets during the spring. The less compact cultivars are to be preferred as they make more slender growth which associates much better with, for example, winter- and spring-flowering pansies. 'Royal Blue', 'Tall Blue' and 'Rosea' with soft pink flowers are all ideal. Seed is sown in July. Sun; upright; top.

Narcissus Daffodils do not come immediately to mind for inclusion in a list of hanging basket subjects but the shorter growing cultivars perform very well. They can be planted in the top or sides especially with plants such as winter-flowering pansies and ivies to give a pleasing display in the spring. 'Hawera', 'Jack Snipe' and 'Sugar Bush' are all good examples as they grow under 30 cm (12 in.) high. Sun or semi-shade; upright; top.

Osteospermum Cultivars can be used in larger hanging baskets. The daisy-like flowers are white, pink, purple or yellow. 'Whirligig' has grey-green foliage with the palest blue flowers which shade to a light grey; the outer ray florets are unusual in that they have their edges folded inwards mid-way and then expand again at the tips. Some of the best cultivars include 'Blue Streak', white and blue; 'Tresco Purple'; 'Hopleys', pink; and 'Silver Sparkler', white with variegated foliage. They are all half hardy and sun lovers. Stem cuttings are best rooted in autumn. Sun; semi-trailing; top or filler.

Pelargonium Frequently but erroneously referred to as geraniums, the two main types used in hanging baskets are the zonal and ivy-leaved hybrids. Both types are sun lovers. The latter are particularly suited to hanging baskets as their growth is pendulous and flowering virtually continuous. Fairly recently a small flowered group of ivy-leaved pelargoniums, has become popular; these are known as Mini Cascades which are capable of very profuse flowering ranging from pink, lilac and red. 'L'Elégante' is an extremely good variegated cultivar with leaves that take on a pinkish tinge in full sun.

Zonal pelargoniums usually have a stiffer habit of growth than ivy-leaved pelargoniums and are best used as main central subjects in a mixed planting. Variegated- and coloured-foliaged cultivars give added interest. Some like 'Platinum' have deep pink flowers and white variegated leaves; 'Golden Harry Hieover' has red flowers and small light gold-green leaves and has a pink-flowered variant; 'Frank Headley' with pink flowers and white-variegated foliage has quite lax growth and therefore makes an ideal basket subject. All the above are propagated from cuttings in autumn. There are, however, a wide range of colours available from seed. The so-called modern multi-bloom types should do well in baskets as main subjects and although the flower heads are relatively small they are borne profusely and recover quickly after inclement weather. There is just one ivy-leaved, seed-raised cultivar,

An interesting spring display of white narcissi and muscari in wall pots

'Summer Shower', but it does not have a good colour range. Sow seed in early autumn or spring in a temperature of 23°C (74°F). The seedlings also need to be grown on in warmth, particularly for the later sowings. Sun; upright or trailing; side or top (see p. 63).

Petunia Modern cultivars have been bred to give weather resistance as well as the wide range of vibrant colours of this popular subject. They are raised from seed but a new introduction, Surfinia, is produced from cuttings and makes very large cascading plants; as yet the colour range is somewhat limited but it is inevitable that this will improve. The Cloud series are particularly good. As a single subject petunias make a striking feature, but they also associate well with other plants. Sow seed in March in gentle heat. Sun; upright or trailing; side or top.

Polygonum capitatum An easily raised plant from seed sown in February or March. It is virtually hardy but to be on the safe side needs to be propagated each year. The pink flowers are formed in small globular heads which are produced profusely throughout the summer and autumn. The small evergreen foliage is distinctly marked with a bronze echelon. Sun; trailing; side or filler.

Portulaca grandiflora An annual succulent with exquisitely coloured flowers including reds, pinks, oranges, yellow, cream and white. There are single and semi-double forms. Seed should be sown in spring in warmth. Sun; semi-trailing; side.

Primula Primula acaulis and P. × polyanthus can both be used in a mixed planting for spring display; white, yellow, pink, red and blue flowers are freely borne. Seed must be sown in the spring or early summer so that good-sized plants are available for planting up in the early autumn to establish well in baskets. Sun or semi-shade; upright; top.

Scaevola aemula This is a recent introduction which has made a tremendous impact both as a single subject and in mixed plantings. Its pendent stems are covered continually in blue fan-shaped flowers. The cultivar most commonly available is one called 'Blue Wonder'. It is also recommended for growing under glass. Propagation is by stem cuttings in spring and autumn using a heated propagator. Sun; semi-trailing; side, top or filler.

Tagetes The African and French marigolds are valuable summer-flowering plants with their bright yellow, orange or bronze

A popular combination of mixed petunias, impatiens and pelargoniums

flowers. Although the larger-flowered types are useful as a main central subject in a hanging basket, the smaller-flowered cultivars mix better with other plants. There is a bewildering number of cultivars to choose from with hybrids between *T. erecta* (African marigold) and *T. patula* (French marigold) to add to the choice, not to mention *T. tenuifolia* often sold as *T. signata*. The latter makes fairly dense plants with masses of small flowers. Seed should be sown in March in gentle heat. Sun; upright; top.

Thunbergia alata This plant gets its popular name black-eyed Susan from the usually black-centred flowers, although the cultivar 'Susie' always lacks the central black disc. The white, yellow or orange flowers are held on long thin trailing and climbing stems. Flowering commences in early summer and continues through to the beginning of autumn. It makes a good single subject for a hanging basket but needs to be used sparingly in a mixed planting as its scrambling, twining growth can overcrowd other plants. Seed is sown in February or March. Sun; trailing; side.

Thymophylla tenuiloba Small yellow, single, daisy-like flowers of the golden fleece are produced in great profusion. Easily raised from seed sown in spring in warmth. Sun; trailing; side, top or filler.

Tropaeolum majus Popularly called nasturtium, this trailing or semi-trailing annual is a perfect basket plant. It is however prone to attack by blackfly and can also attract cabbage white butterfly caterpillars. Single and double flowers come in cream, yellow, orange or red. There are more compact selections such as the double-flowered Gleam series and Whirlybird series. 'Alaska' has variegated foliage and the usual range of flower colours (see p. 6). Nasturtiums should be sown in small pots putting two seeds in a container and then thinning down to one plant. 'Hermine Grashoff' has double orange-red flowers and can be propagated only from stem cuttings taken in February.

Tropaeolum peregrinum, the Canary creeper, has bright lemon-yellow flowers and makes long trailing growths. It is best suited to larger baskets. Sun; upright or trailing; side or top.

Verbena × hybrida There are two main groups of this attractive plant, one raised from cuttings, the other from seed. In the latter the more lax growing cultivars should be used for hanging baskets;

Thunbergia alata 'Sundance'

'Romance Hybrids' and 'Showtime' are ideal, and they both have a good range of colours from white to pink, red, purple and violet. Seed should be sown in early spring in heat.

Those raised from cuttings need to be rooted in the autumn and over-wintered in frost-free conditions. The following are the best cultivars: 'Lawrence Johnstone', bright red; 'Loveliness', pale lavender; 'Mme du Barry', deep pink; 'Silver Anne' (sometimes known as 'Pink Bouquet'), pale pink shading to a deeper colour; 'Sissinghurst', magenta; and 'White Knight'. Sun; upright or trailing; side or top (see p. 11).

Vinca The periwinkles *Vinca major* and *V. minor* both make a good display in winter and spring. The evergreen foliage, further enhanced in the variegated cultivars, is held on slender trailing stems. There are many variants of both periwinkles with single or double, white, blue or purple flowers appearing in late winter and spring. *V. minor* with its smaller leaves is very hardy and is best for hanging baskets in an exposed situation. Propagation is by cuttings which can be taken at any time, and also by removing rooted layers in autumn for spring. Sun or shade; trailing; side or top.

Viola × wittrockiana This is a very complex hybrid that has given rise to the garden pansies. The winter-flowering cultivars are especially suitable for hanging baskets, as in mild weather flowering occurs even during the dull winter months and is profuse in the spring. As a single subject, pansies are ideal, coming as they do in fairly strong colours. The Crystal Bowl Hybrids and Universal Hybrids have become extremely popular. Seed needs to be sown in midsummer and the plants grown on in as cool conditions as possible, preferably in small containers.

Of all the introductions of *V. cornuta*, the small-flowered pansy, the Princess Series is quite outstanding. Masses of flowers of either blue, cream or purple are produced even in the winter during favourable weather conditions. Sun or semi-shade; upright; side or top (see p. 17).

Plants for the Greenhouse and Conservatory

Hanging baskets can be enjoyed in the conservatory, greenhouse and the home, as well as outside. The additional protection gained by growing plants under cover means that a display will last for longer but also that more tender plants can be used. The best of these are described below.

A warm or, as it is sometimes referred to, a temperate greenhouse is one that is maintained at a night minimum temperature of 10°C (50°F). It can be regarded generally as the best environment for the majority of plants suitable for hanging baskets listed below. A cool greenhouse with a minimum night temperature of 5°C (40°F) is useful but plants requiring warmer treatment, although tolerating the lower temperature, will not give of their best.

A cold greenhouse has no supplementary heating but in summer it is capable of providing adequate conditions for a wide range of plants that require heat in winter. Only a very limited range of hardy plants can be expected to thrive all through the year out of doors, so benefit from the protection of unheated glass during the coldest weather.

Most plants in greenhouses or conservatories will require shading in late spring and summer and possibly on into the autumn. This applies particularly to such plants as achimenes, begonias, orchids, ferns and streptocarpus. Pelargoniums and bougainvilleas revel in good light and heat, but in high summer even these benefit from the use of slatted blinds or the light shading afforded by a proprietary 'white wash' shading paint or meshed fabric fastened to the greenhouse or conservatory frame.

In the home the main deciding factor is usually light, or perhaps, lack of it, as any plant more than 2 m (6 ft) from a natural light source is likely to become etiolated and weak. Conversely too much light in spring and high summer, such as experienced hanging by a window facing full south, can spoil a display. For in excessively high temperatures foliage plants invariably bleach and flowering plants have a shorter time in bloom than in a shadier position.

Acalypha hispida **'Hispaniola'** At its best in a warm greenhouse, this plant has short tassels of light red flowers which hang on fairly short, slender stems. Flowering continues over a long period and only in the depth of winter is it likely to lack colour. A single plant in a small basket looks very attractive but an even better display is achieved by planting several in a large container. Cuttings root at any time of the year.

Achimenes Many species and cultivars of the hot water plant are available with flower colours from white, pink, red, blue and deep purple. The small scaly rhizomes should be planted in seed trays or shallow pots using a fibrous potting compost. This should be done in the spring and a temperature of at least 18°C (65°F) must be maintained. Watering must be done sparingly until active growth is achieved. Before the plants have become too well established they should be planted in small wire hanging baskets. It pays to insert some in the sides to give a well-furnished display. As soon as the plants have rooted into the new compost the growing tips can be pinched out to encourage a bushier plant. Flowering can be

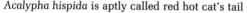

Acalypha hispida is aptly called red hot cat's tail

48

Left: *Achimenes* 'Harveyi'. Right: *Aeschynanthus speciosus*

expected to commence in midsummer and continue for many weeks. When flowering ceases water should be withheld to induce dormancy when the rhizomes should be kept in cool conditions. Recently at least two seed-raised cultivars have been introduced. Seed sown in March will produce flowering plants during August.

Achimenes longiflora has violet blue flowers. Cultivars include 'Alba', white; 'Major', lavender; and 'Paul Arnold', purple with white throat. Other hybrids are available in a wide range of colours.

× *Achimenantha naegelioides* An intergeneric hybrid between *Achimenes* and *Smithiantha* giving rise to flowers of pink, white and red, often with spotting. They are raised in the same way as that described for *Achimenes* (above).

Aeschynanthus The many species and cultivars are fairly easily grown in a warm greenhouse. Plenty of water is required in the growing season but care must be taken during the winter. They respond to regular feeding but this should be much reduced as the season progresses into duller, cooler weather. Propagation is by short stem cuttings taken in spring or summer and placed in a heated propagator with bottom heat.

Alsobia dianthiflora White flowers with deeply fringed petals held on long pendulous stems are not too freely borne but are very attractive. Stem cuttings root easily in a heated propagator during spring and summer.

Asparagus densiflorus **'Sprengeri'** Commonly referred to as a fern although, in fact, it belongs to the lily family. This foliage plant makes a good single subject for greenhouse and the home. It is a tough plant and can withstand a certain amount of neglect. However, to obtain good large specimens copious watering and regular feeding is necessary. Excessive direct sunlight will cause a yellowing of the otherwise bright green feathery foliage. It is easily increased by division or from seed sown in heat (17–20°C/62–68°F) in spring or early summer (see p. 8).

Begonia The large-flowered, pendulous types are particularly good in a greenhouse. Several tuberous rooted cultivars are available and are usually grown as single plant specimens. 'Crimson Cascade', 'Gold Cascade', 'Orange Cascade' and 'Lou-Anne', with pale rose-pink flowers, are readily obtained. The tubers are started into growth in a fibrous compost in heat and subsequently planted in medium-sized baskets by late spring. Flowering will continue from midsummer until the autumn when tubers must be gradually dried off to induce dormancy ready for starting into growth the following spring. Begonias can also be raised from seed sown in heat (20°C/68°F). *B. sutherlandii* has already been described (see p. 29) and is particularly fine when given the protection of a greenhouse.

Begonia solananthera is one of the few begonias with slightly fragrant flowers. These are white with internal red markings and appear in winter and spring. The trailing stems are fairly well furnished with small blooms. Propagation is by stem cuttings in spring or summer.

Begonia rex Cultorum Hybrids are a rather complex group grown for their very attractively marked foliage. Although the plants are rather low growing and not at all trailing they still make ideal small or medium basket plants as the large leaves tend to envelope and disguise the container.

Bougainvillea This well-known plant with its coloured bracts is not an obvious choice for a basket, but the smaller growing cultivars can be very accommodating. In particular *B. glabra* 'Variegata' with its cream and green foliage and pale magenta bracts makes a fine show over a very long period. Semi-hardwood and hardwood cuttings will root with some difficulty in the spring using a heated

---

Begonia sutherlandii is suitable for growing in baskets indoors or outside

51

Left: *Bougainvillea glabra*. Right: *Browallia speciosa* 'White Troll'

propagator. Smaller, thinner cuttings of softer growth taken in summer seem to root more readily.

Browallia speciosa Generally grown as a pot plant this attractive plant is equally well suited to a hanging basket especially when planted in the sides as well as the top. It is easily raised from seed sown in gentle heat (15–20°C/62–68°F) in the spring. Having pricked out the seedlings into trays or, preferably, small pots, they can be subsequently planted in baskets. Flowering will commence in midsummer and continue until late autumn. 'Blue Troll' is a clear blue; 'White Troll' white; 'Heavenly Bells' sky blue; and 'Vanja' deep blue with a white eye.

The smaller-flowered B. *viscosa* is also good and is grown in just the same way as described above. 'Sapphire' has intense blue flowers with a small white eye.

Campanula isophylla A charming white- or blue-flowered subject for small hanging baskets, and as it tolerates quite cool conditions it is ideal even in a less heated greenhouse. Raise from seed sown in the spring or early summer at a temperature of 15–20°C (62–68°F), and flowering plants should be available the following year. Plants can also be divided. 'Kristal Hybrids', 'Stella Blue' and 'Stella White' are recommended cultivars.

Centradenia inaequilateralis 'Cascade' A recent introduction with clear pink flowers best suited for growing in a small basket in warmth. Stem cuttings should be rooted in summer or seed sown in spring at a temperature of 20°C (68°F).

× **Codonantanthus** This is an intergeneric cross between *Codonanthe* and *Nematanthus*. Several good trailing plants have been produced: namely 'Antique Gold', yellow flowers and glossy green foliage; 'Rosy Dawn', flower tube pink, yellow lobes; and 'Tambourine', rosy tube and yellow lobes, constantly in bloom. New plants can be raised from cuttings taken in spring or summer.

Chlorophytum comosum 'Variegatum' Arguably the most popular of all the variegated foliage plants and already described as an out-door summer subject on page 31. However, with protection it is possible to develop very large specimens because the flower spikes produce small plantlets at their tips which in turn grow out to give further pendulous growth. It is particularly suitable for the home and looks especially fine in a container held up by macramé. Propagation is by division or by potting up small flower stem plantlets at any time. For smaller baskets *C. comosum* 'Vittatum' is more compact and therefore neater in growth (see p. 37).

Ceropegia lineans subsp. woodii The common names, hearts entangled, sweetheart vine and hearts on a string, aptly describe this plant with its extremely slender stems and fleshy, somewhat heart-shaped leaves. The small tubular flowers are dark purple and are more curious than beautiful, but the foliage is sea green with purple and grey-green markings and purple undersides. An extremely attractive variegated cultivar is also available. Small tubers formed on the stems can be removed in spring or summer and grown on to increase numbers.

Coelogyne cristata One of the best orchids for beginners, it is quite happy in cool conditions and makes a good basketful of growth in time. The flowers are white with deep yellow markings and appear in the winter to early spring. There are several variants. Watering and regular misting with a hand-held spray is necessary when in full growth. *C. massangeana* and *C. speciosa* are two species worth growing, but require somewhat warmer conditions. Propagation is by division after flowering (see p. 4).

Dendrobium nobile Another orchid that is easy to grow. The long pseudobulbs tend to bend over so making this species a good basket subject. Flowering freely from January to April, the white and rosy pink blooms are very attractive. There are many variations including one with pure white flowers. Although requiring some warmth in the growing season, cooler conditions are perfectly adequate together with much less water during the resting period. Propagation is by division as new growth appears.

Davallia canariensis A true fern which remains evergreen and is quite adaptable to room conditions. The long main stems are covered with brown scales and give rise to the common name of Hare's foot fern. The plant will withstand dryness at the root provided the fronds are sprayed with clear water. Even in a small basket, a quite large specimen can result. A cool greenhouse is quite adequate for this subject. Careful division of the main stem in spring is the easiest form of propagation.

Duchesnea indica Allied to the strawberry, this plant, although not outstanding, produces long trailing growths and mid-green foliage. It is quite hardy and can therefore be regarded as a tough subject for a cold greenhouse or an unheated room, corridor or entrance porch. The flowers are yellow followed by strawberry-like fruits which are scarcely edible. Propagate by runners or raise from seed at a temperature of 15–20°C (62–68°F).

Epiphyllum Several hybrids are in cultivation with white, pink or red flowers. This epiphytic cactus requires a fairly large basket to support rather heavy, flat, succulent stems. Cuttings root quite readily in summer.

Epipremnum aureum Usually seen as a climbing plant but making an acceptable basket subject. The yellow or cream variegated leaves are held on long similarly marked trailing stems. E. aureum 'Marble Queen' has boldly white-streaked, mid-green foliage. Warm greenhouse conditions are ideal but epipremnum makes a tolerably good house plant. Stem cuttings root quite readily in spring or summer.

Episcia cupreata Although there are many other species and a number of cultivars, E. cupreata is as good as any to grow. The bronzy foliage helps to set off orange flowers. It pays to propagate regularly using cuttings of young growths. Several plants in a basket will ensure a good display. A warm humid greenhouse is really required to bring the plants to perfection. Softwood stem cuttings root readily in spring and summer.

Ficus pumila The small-leaved trailing fig should be grown as a single subject in a small basket as it is not too rampant. Some

Episcia cupreata 'Silver Sheen'

cultivars have either silver or gold variegation and tend to be even less strong growing. Stem cuttings should be rooted in a warm propagator in spring or summer (see p. 23).

Gibasis pellucida More popularly known as *Tradescantia* 'Bridal Veil'. Best grown as a single subject when the myriads of small white flowers held on wiry stems make a continual display over many months. Cuttings are easily rooted at any time of the year.

Hatiora salicornioides The tiny tufts of yellow flowers always cause comment. It is a much branched succulent plant and is able to withstand a certain amount of drying out, although humidity and plenty of water ensure a good specimen. Short cuttings from the succulent stems root quite easily in summer on an open greenhouse bench or room window sill.

Hypoestes phyllostachya 'Bettina'

Hoya lanceolata subsp. bella Invariably referred to as just *Hoya bella*, this is a beautiful free-flowering summer-basket subject. It is very sweetly scented and because of the downward facing clusters of flowers the plant needs to be in an elevated situation for them to be shown off to advantage. The root system is not strong so a small basket is neccessary and, for the same reason, careful watering is essential especially in the dull winter months. Occasional feeding is important to achieve a healthy plant. Propagate from stem cuttings in spring or late summer.

Hypoestes phyllostachya Commonly and aptly called the polka dot plant as the dark green leaves are splashed with either white or deep pink. It is best grown in small baskets although a massed planting in a larger container can look very striking. Although cuttings root very readily at any time it is very easily raised from seed sown in warmth, 20°C (68°F), in spring or early summer as the resultant plants come true to type.

Impatiens repens This is a perfect basket plant even though its flowering can be a little capricious. Dark green foliage held on long trailing, somewhat fleshy stems provides a pleasant contrast to the clear yellow flowers. Propagate from cuttings in spring and

Kalanchoe manginii

summer. *I. walleriana*, already described for outdoor baskets on page 37, can be brought to perfection when given protection. Stem cuttings taken in spring or summer and placed in a propagator or even under a polythene bag root with ease. Seed can also be sown in spring and early summer.

Kalanchoe manginii A superb winter-flowering succulent plant. As a single subject in a small basket it is attractive but when several plants are grown in a large container the result can be spectacular. Raised from cuttings in early summer, flowering can be expected in the first year and if the old flowering growth is cut back a more profuse display is ensured for the following year. Regular watering and feeding is necessary during the growing season. The tubular flowers are red but a newer hybrid *K*. 'Tessa' is orange.

Lachenalia The South African cowslip has nothing to do with the primula family and is in fact liliaceous. It is an excellent bulbous plant for the cool or temperate greenhouse for winter and spring flowering. Plant fairly thickly in a wire or wooden hanging basket for a massed display of yellow flowers on firm but somewhat slender stems. The flowers are further enhanced by strap-like leaves which in some forms have bronze-purple blotches. Dormant bulbs need to be planted in August. The main species available are *Lachenelia aloides* and its varieties *aurea* and *quadricolor*.

Large numbers of bulbs can be obtained by removing the many small bulblets that are produced round a mature parent bulb. The bulblets are planted in boxes and grown on for one or two years until they reach flowering size. Mature leaves, when severed cleanly, inserted into sandy compost and placed in a heated propagator, will also produce bulblets on the leaf base. Seed can be sown as soon as it is ripe; seedlings often flower within two years. After flowering the plants need to be kept fed and watered until foliage begins to die back naturally at which time watering must be gradually withheld and the bulbs allowed to become quite dormant.

Lantana montevidensis This is a tender plant that revels in full sun. The rosy lilac to violet flowers are produced very freely over a long period and as they are borne on slender growths easy intermingling is achieved. Cuttings need to be rooted in autumn or very early spring. It can also be used out of doors (see p. 38).

Nepenthes × *hookeriana*, one of the pitcher plants

Mimulus × hybridus Although the musk has been described for out-door hanging baskets on page 38, it makes a fine single subject specimen for a cool greenhouse from an autumn sowing. Alternatively seed can be sown in spring. One plant is capable of enveloping a 30 cm (12 in.) basket when grown on to flower in spring.

Nepenthes To grow pitcher plants well it is necessary to be able to provide warmth and high humidity together with plenty of moisture at the root. Liquid fertilizer is beneficial which can be applied as a foliar feed. Old plants can be cut hard back in the spring. Compost must be well drained. There are many species and hybrids available but all have curious, but mostly attractive, 'pitchers' which are formed as a modification to the leaf and act as insect traps. Propagation is best achieved by layering, although cuttings can be rooted in spring.

Nephrolepis *Nephrolepis cordifolia*, the ladder fern, and *N. exaltata*, the Boston fern, are very good house plants but, of course, do well in greenhouses and conservatories where they are capable of making quite large single specimens. Division in spring or summer is the easiest method of increase.

Pelargonium Although already described for flowering out of doors in the summer (see p. 41) the many cultivars available, especially the ivy-leaf type, are admirably suited for growing in a heated greenhouse or conservatory to extend their flowering season. Raise from cuttings at any time. Sow seed in spring at a temperature of 15–20°C (62–68°F).

Philodendron scandens Usually grown as an indoor climber, it also makes a very acceptable basket plant. Long pendent stems bear heart-shaped glossy leaves. Semi-shaded areas are ideal. The red-leaved philodendron, *P. erubescens*, is an interesting species worth growing. Cuttings root readily in spring and summer.

Phlebodium aureum (*Polypodium aureum*) The grey-green fronds of this fern can grow to a considerable length, 1 m (39 in.), making an impressive basket plant for a warm greenhouse. Easily increased by division, this can also be raised from spores in summer.

Platycerium The common names of staghorn fern, elkhorn fern and antelope fern, give an immediate indication of the shape of the divided fronds. Although *Platycerium* species are best grown on slabs of bark, the common *P. bifurcatum* seems to be quite happy in a small hanging basket which will be completely enveloped by the

Left: *Russelia equisetiformis*. Right: *Senecio rowleyanus*

plant, provided irrigation, feeding and regular misting with clear water is carried out. Propagate by removing the young plantlets which form on the roots.

Plectranthus oertendahlii Swedish ivy is an easily grown subject and is capable of tolerating a wide range of growing conditions. The dark green leaves with silver veining have scalloped margins and are purple beneath. Growth is quite pendent. Stem cuttings seem to root easily at any time although in the winter months propagation will be slower.

Rhodochiton atrosanguineum Generally grown as a climbing plant in the cool greenhouse, the interesting and attractive pendent flowers are seen to advantage if used in a hanging basket. Seed should be sown, if possible, as fresh as possible to ensure good germination. If sown in the spring in a temperature of 15°C (62°F) it will flower by late summer and can then be grown on for several years. Water with great care in the winter.

Russelia equisetiformis When grown well the fountain plant or fire cracker plant is virtually in continuous flower. The drooping stems and branchlets are leafless producing scarlet tubular flowers. *Russelia* will put up with a certain amount of neglect and tolerates cool but frost-free conditions. A sunny or lightly shaded spot is ideal. Cuttings root quite readily in spring and summer in a heated propagator.

Schlumbergera × buckleyi There are many hybrids of the so called Christmas cactus and Easter cactus. Although generally bought as small pot plants they make fine basket subjects if grown in a small container. Best grown in a minimum temperature of 10°C (50°F), with shade through the hottest days of summer. Regular watering and feeding is required in the growing season but must be much reduced in winter and the plant rested in the late summer. Stem sections should be rooted in the summer.

Sedum morganianum The pendulous growths have very succulent, glaucous leaves arranged spirally. These overlap each other giving rise to the common name of donkey's tail. The pink flowers are held on pendent stalks but add little to the attractiveness of the plant. It makes a good plant for a warm sunny situation in the home, but is also suited to cool conditions. Short lengths of stem can be rooted in spring or summer.

Senecio rowleyanus Aptly called string-of-beads because of the small globose foliage growing on extremely slender stems extending to some considerable length. It is suitable for a frost-free greenhouse or as a house plant in a sunny position. Short lengths of the stem root readily in spring or summer (see p. 60).

Solenostemon scutellarioides More familiarly known as *Coleus blumei*, this species has several cultivars suitable for hanging baskets. The best is 'Lord Falmouth', with small heart-shaped green leaves with pink centres and bronze veining. 'Picturatum' has similarly shaped leaves but crimson-brown in colour. 'Bizarre Croton', 'Laing's Croton', 'Red Croton' all have narrow leaves but more compact growth. Coleus are only suitable for growing under glass and require warmth during the winter. Cuttings root readily in spring and summer. Raise from seed sown in spring at a temperature of 20°C (68°F).

Stenotaphrum secundatum 'Variegatum' An ornamental grass for the warm greenhouse or conservatory. It is a fairly rapid grower so care must be taken when mixing with other subjects and for that reason it is best grown alone. Cuttings are easily rooted at any time of the year.

Streptocarpus Several species make excellent basket subjects but some of the hybrids when planted in the top and sides can make a particularly stunning display. Among the hybrids the seed-raised cultivars such as 'Concorde' and those vegetatively propagated such as 'Helen' and 'Lisa' are particularly good. Of the species S. *caulescens* and S. *saxorum* are excellent with their profusion of small blue flowers; the latter has somewhat succulent leaves. S. *kirkii* is a fairly upright bushy grower but if also planted in the sides will furnish a medium-sized basket.

Warmth is necessary to grow streptocarpus well in winter and spring. Good, but not direct, sunlight is important to ensure adequate flowering. Seed should be sown in the spring and germinated at 25 °C (77 °F) when the plants will flower in July and August. Cuttings will root readily in a warm propagator in spring and summer.

Schlumbergera × *buckleyi*, the Christmas cactus

Pelargonium 'Amethyst' (see pp. 41 and 59)

Tradescantia fluminensis There are various forms of this popular greenhouse subject and house plant. The white- and yellow-variegated forms are ubiquitous. Far less common is the most attractive *T. fluminesis* 'Tricolor Minima' which deserves to be more widely grown. Its smaller leaves are variegated pink, white and green making it much less rampant than the more common types. A recent introduction called *T.* 'Maiden Blush' has considerable promise; the leaves at the top of the stems have cream variegation flushed deep pink at their very tips. However, the plant does seem to go into a period in summer when the foliage is less striking but nevertheless is still well worth growing. *T. zebrina* (formerly *Z. pendula*) is a strong growing subject with green and purple leaves usually striped with silver and with purple undersides. Tradescantias are easily raised from stem cuttings taken at any time during the year.

Tradescantia see also **Gibasis**

Index

Page numbers in **bold** type refer to illustrations

Acalypha 47–8
  hispida **48**
× Achimenantha 49
Achimenes 47, 48
  'Harveyi' **49**
Aechynanthus 49
  speciosus **49**
Ageratum 28
Alsobia 49–50
Argyranthemum
    (marguerite, Paris
    daisy) 28
  'Jamaica Primrose' 28, **29**
Asparagus densiflorus
    'Sprengeri' **8**, 51
Aucuba 28

Begonia 16, 28–9, 47, 51
  sutherlandii 29, **50**, 51
Bidens 29
Bougainvillea 47, 51–2
  glabra **52**
Brachycome (Swan River
    daisy) 29
Browallia 52
  speciosa 'White Troll' 52,
    52

Calceolaria 30
Campanula **11**, 30, 52
Centradenia 53
Ceropegia 53
Chlorophytum (spider plant)
    10, 31, **37**, 53
Chrysanthemum see
    Argyranthemum
× Codonanthanthus 53
Coelogyne 53
  cristata **4**, 53
Coleus see Solenostemon
Convolvulus 31
  sabatius 31, **31**
cucumber 27

Davallia 54
Dendrobium 53–4
Dorotheanthus bellidiformis
    31, 32
Duchesnea 54

Ephiphyllum 54
Epipremnum 54
Episcia 54
  cupreata 'Silver Sheen' **55**

Erica (winter heath) 32
Erigeron 32

Felicia 32
  amelloides 'Variegata' 32,
    33
ferns 54, 57, 59
Ficus 54–5
Fuchsia 32, 34–5
  'Auntie Jinks' **33**, 34
Gazania ringens
    (G. splendens) **34**, 35
Gibasis 55
Glechoma 35

Hatiora 55
heathers 25
Hebe 35
Hedera (ivy) 35, **37**
Helichrysum 23, 35–6
herbs **17**, 27
Hoya 56
Hypoestes 54
  phyllostachya 'Bettina' **56**,
    56

Impatiens (busy lizzie) 16,
    37, **37**, **43**, 56–7
Ipomoea (morning glory) 37

Kalanchoe 57
  manginii 57, **57**

Lachenalia 57–8
Lamium 38
Lantana 38
  montevidensis **36**, 38, 58
Lathyrus 38
Lobelia **1**, 24, **23**, 38
Lotus **10**, 38

Mesembryanthemum see
    Dorotheanthus
Mimulus, 38, 59
  moschatus 'Viva' **39**
Muscari (grape hyacinth)
    39, **40**
Myosotis (forget-me-not) 39

Narcissus (daffodil) 25, **40**,
    41
Nemesia 39
Nepenthes (pitcher plant) 59
  × hookeriana **58**
Nephrolepsis 59

orchids 47, 53
Osteospermum 41

parsley **13**, 27
Pelargonium 23, 24, 41, **43**,
    47
  'Amethyst' **63**
  Balcon Series **11**
Petunia **23**, 42, **43**
Philodendron 59
Phlebodium 59
Platycerium 59–60
Plectostachys see
    Helichrysum
Plectranthus 60
Polygonum 42
Polypodium see Phlebodium
Portulaca 42
Primula 42

Rhodochiton 60
Russellia 61
  equisetiformis **60**

Scaevola 42
Schlumbergera × buckleyi
    61, **62**
Sedum 61
Senecio rowleyanus **60**, 61
Solenostemon 61
Stenotaphrum 62
strawberry 27
Streptocarpus 47, 62

Tagetes (African and
    French marigolds)
    42–3
Thunbergia 45
  alata 'Sundance' **44**
Thymophylla 45
tomatoes **14**, 27, **27**
Tradescantia 63, see also
    Gibasis
Tropaeolum (nasturtium)
    12, 45
  majus 'Alaska' **6**, 45

Verbena 45–6
  'Sissinghurst' **10**, 46
Vinca (periwinkle) 46
Viola (pansies) 16, **17**, 25,
    46